Oil Power

BY PATTI RICHARDS

Stride
An Imprint of The Child's World®
childsworld.com

The Child's World®
childsworld.com

Published by The Child's World®
800-599-READ • childsworld.com

Photography Credits
Photographs ©: Shutterstock Images, cover, 1, 6, 7, 10, 14,
19, 20, 23, 24, 26; Morph Art Creation/Shutterstock Images,
5; Rafa Irusta/Shutterstock Images, 8; Red Line Editorial,
9; Alizada Studios/Shutterstock Images, 13; Sinchai B./
Shutterstock Images, 15; Colin Seddon/Shutterstock Images, 16;
Jacob Lund/iStockphoto, 25; iStockphoto, 28

ISBN Information
9781503865020 (Reinforced Library Binding)
9781503866003 (Portable Document Format)
9781503866843 (Online Multi-user eBook)
9781503867680 (Electronic Publication)

LCCN 2022939528

Printed in the United States of America

ABOUT THE AUTHOR

Patti Richards has spent more
than 30 years writing stories and
telling tales. She is the author of
one fiction and four nonfiction
books for kids. She is part of an
award-winning poetry anthology
and also writes for children's
magazines. Richards lives in
Farmington Hills, Michigan, with
her husband, Gene.

Contents

CHAPTER ONE

Oil Underground

Long before European explorers came to North America, the Seneca Nation lived in what is now Pennsylvania. They raised crops, hunted, and fished. They had a close relationship with Earth. This meant they were always looking for new ways to use the gifts from nature. Around the year 1410, they found a dark material coming up from the ground. The Seneca people gathered this thick, waxy substance. They used it as a body paint, insect repellent, and for fires. They also used it as a medicine. Today, people call this substance oil. It is a common source of energy.

Oil is hidden deep within the ground. It is found between layers of rock. Oil is a **fossil fuel**. It takes millions of years for fossil fuels to form. They are made from very old animal and plant remains. These things were buried underground. They experienced a lot of pressure and heat.

Pennsylvania was one of the first places where people drilled wells for underground oil. The first oil well was built there in 1859.

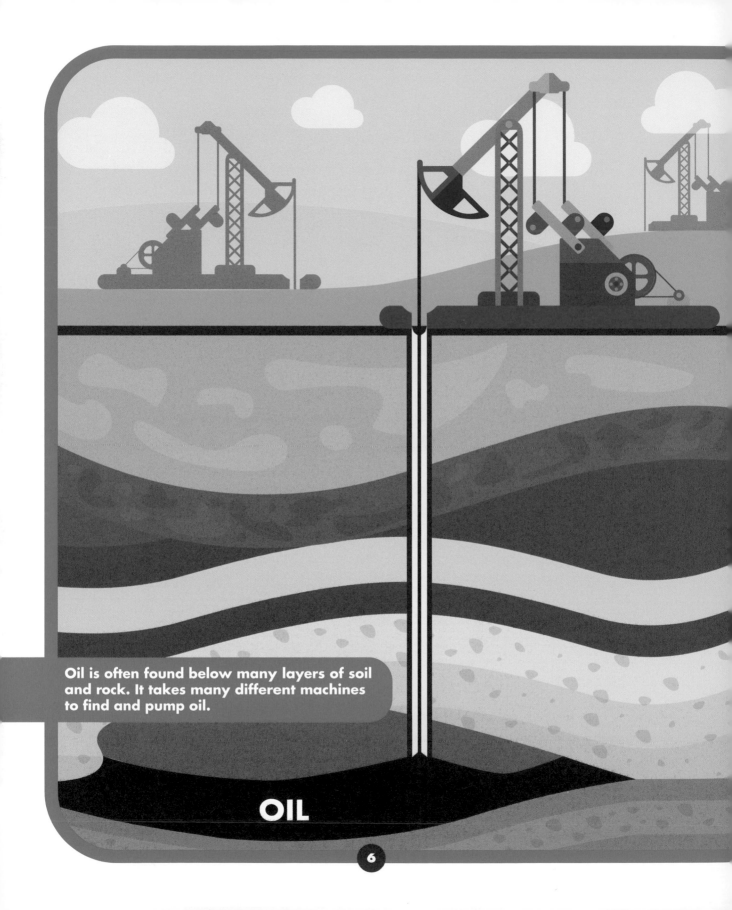

Oil is often found below many layers of soil and rock. It takes many different machines to find and pump oil.

OIL

Some of these remains eventually became oil.

Typically, people must dig up oil in order to get it. Some people work on oil rigs. These are structures near oil wells. They can be in the sea or on land. Oil rigs have machines that drill into the ground. They take out oil. Afterward, people must transport it. They may load it into a truck or train. Other times, oil is moved through **pipelines**. Sometimes oil needs to be transported across the ocean. People use oil tankers to do this. These are large ships.

LEADING OIL PRODUCERS

Starting in 2018, the United States removed more oil from below Earth's surface than any other country. People got it from the land and U.S.-controlled waters. Oil in the United States came from 32 states. Most of the oil came from five U.S. states: Texas, North Dakota, New Mexico, Oklahoma, and Colorado. The United States is not the only country that searches for oil. In 2020, Russia, Saudi Arabia, Iraq, and Canada were also large oil producers.

Oil is used to make the fuel that runs airplanes and other vehicles.

Oil is very energy dense. That means it stores more energy by **volume** than the same amount of some other substances. Some people use oil's energy to create electricity. They may burn oil to make steam. The steam moves **turbines** that make electricity. This electricity is then brought to people's homes and communities.

However, oil is used for more than just making electricity. It is also used to power airplanes and vehicles. People use oil to make things such as plastics and cleaning chemicals.

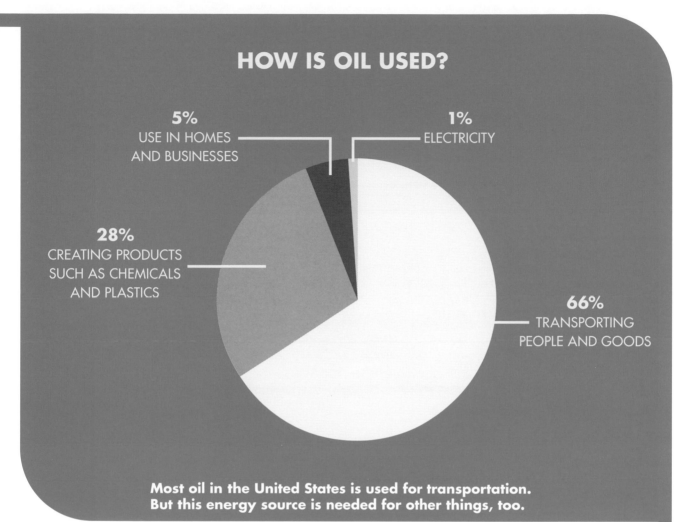

HOW IS OIL USED?

5%
USE IN HOMES
AND BUSINESSES

1%
ELECTRICITY

28%
CREATING PRODUCTS
SUCH AS CHEMICALS
AND PLASTICS

66%
TRANSPORTING
PEOPLE AND GOODS

**Most oil in the United States is used for transportation.
But this energy source is needed for other things, too.**

Oil in its natural state is called crude oil. When crude oil is **distilled**, other energy-rich products remain. One of these is gasoline. Gasoline is used to power cars, planes, boats, and other forms of transportation. Gasoline is the most common use for oil.

Home heating oil is another product made from oil. It is one way to heat homes during the cold months.

When a car uses gasoline, it gives off pollution from its tailpipe.

People use home heating oil in furnaces, space heaters, and hot-water heaters.

Another product made when oil is processed is asphalt. This is a thick, black substance. When it dries, it is hard like concrete. Asphalt is often used to make and repair roads. It is also used for roofs. Some batteries even have asphalt in them.

Oil is an important source of energy. It is also needed to make certain products. But oil is not always good for the environment. People need to drill deep underground to find oil. This may hurt land and water **habitats**. Sometimes large oil spills happen. This pollutes the environment. Burning fuels made from oil, such as gasoline, hurts the environment, too. But people still rely on oil. In 2021 alone, the United States used approximately 7.22 billion barrels of oil.

CHAPTER TWO

Problems with Oil

Fossil fuels such as oil take a long time to make. They are called nonrenewable resources. That means people cannot replace the fossil fuels they use. There is a fixed amount of them. Once the fossil fuels are all used up, they are gone.

People depend on fossil fuels like oil. More than 80 percent of the energy people around the world use each year comes from fossil fuels. However, using oil can cause problems for the environment. When fossil fuels such as oil are burned, greenhouse gases are released. Greenhouse gases trap heat on Earth. They make the planet warmer. Over time, too many greenhouse gases have made Earth's temperature warmer than it should be. This warming has resulted in **climate change**. Glaciers are melting and sea levels are rising. The planet is getting stronger heat waves.

Many people drill for oil, but there is a limited amount of the substance available underground.

Melting glaciers are one serious side effect of climate change.

Climate change impacts both animals and people. Animal habitats are getting destroyed. Some people's communities are suffering because of the more extreme weather.

Drilling for oil is not good for the environment either. To build an oil rig on land, people need to clear the area. They may destroy animal habitats to do this. When an oil rig is built, a lot of loud noises come with it.

People move to and from the rig. They have loud vehicles and machines. This noise pollution can disrupt animal behaviors such as breeding, communication, and nesting.

Even trying to find oil can hurt animals. To look for oil, people often use machines that push strong shock waves into the ground. The shock waves bounce back, and experts use data from this to figure out where oil may be. But doing this in the ocean can disturb the animals there. It affects the breeding and feeding behaviors of certain animals. Some animals even experience hearing loss.

Offshore oil rigs can harm sea life.

Oil spills are another way this energy source can hurt the environment. The spills happen when oil is being transported from place to place. For instance, oil might be placed in a pipeline or on an oil tanker. Sometimes mistakes or bad equipment cause the oil to leak out. Other times extreme weather, such as hurricanes, cause the spills.

Trained professionals can clean oil off birds, but it is harmful for oil to be on animals in the first place.

The National Oceanic and Atmospheric Administration is a U.S. government group. It works to protect the environment. It says that each year, thousands of oil spills happen in waters near the United States. A lot of these spills are small. They sometimes happen when ships are getting fuel. But any amount of oil in the environment can cause damage. For example, spilled oil may coat plants and animals. A bird that gets oil on its feathers might not be able to fly. A sea otter coated in oil might not be able to keep itself warm. Oil is also poisonous. It can hurt an animal's heart. It could even kill the animal. People can also be hurt by exposure to oil. Their eyes or skin might get irritated. They could develop lung issues, such as wheezing.

THE *EXXON VALDEZ* OIL SPILL

In 1989, the *Exxon Valdez* oil tanker spilled 11 million gallons (41.6 million L) of oil into Alaskan waters. Experts believe 250,000 birds died from the disaster. They also believe the spill killed thousands of sea otters, hundreds of seals and bald eagles, and more than a dozen orcas.

After the spill, the U.S. Congress passed the Oil Pollution Act of 1990. This act makes sure new oil tankers have a double hull, or an extra layer on the outside of the ship. The double hull greatly reduces the amount of oil spilled from ships.

In 2010, one of the worst oil spills happened in the Gulf of Mexico. An oil rig exploded. Four million barrels of oil spilled into the water. It polluted approximately 57,500 square miles (148,924 sq km) of the ocean. It even reached the U.S. coast and polluted beaches and other places there. Experts believe thousands of sea animals died because of the spill. The spill also hurt the animals' habitats.

Workers on oil rigs are also at risk when drilling for oil. Oil can catch fire easily. Sometimes fires start on oil rigs. Pressure might also build up inside an oil well. This pressure may cause an explosion.

Oil wells become unproductive over time. These wells must be properly plugged before people can leave them. Governments have strict steps in place for plugging. If a well is not properly sealed, it can leak fluids and gases. This can make the soil and plant life at the surface unhealthy.

Hydraulic fracturing, or fracking, is one way people bring oil to the surface. In this process, people pump a mixture of water, chemicals, and sand into the ground.

Cleaning up after an oil spill is a messy job.

Many people have spoken out about the risks of fracking.

FRACKING WILL POISON OUR LAND, AIR & WATER

This liquid mixture breaks open layers of rock. Oil and natural gas, another fossil fuel, are released and collected.

People worry that this process might pollute water sources near fracking areas. The Environmental Protection Agency is a U.S. government group. It studied this and found that pollution from fracking could happen. For instance, after the liquid mixture used in fracking cracks open rocks, it becomes wastewater. It needs to be disposed of. Some people put the waste back underground. Others put it in storage tanks. Either way, accidents could cause the dirty water to leak out and hurt the nearby environment.

CHAPTER THREE

The Future of Oil

Oil is a big part of people's lives. It fuels their cars and helps create products they use each day. But oil is not always good for the environment. That is why scientists are looking for, and are already using, new sources of energy. They hope to use energy sources that do not hurt the environment. Finding other ways to get power would greatly reduce the impact oil use has on the environment.

People can help protect both the environment and the world's oil supply by cutting down on their daily use of the substance. Many products come from oil. This includes plastics. Reducing single-use plastics, such as water bottles, can help. People can also buy local products. This cuts down on plastic packaging. It also cuts down on the transportation needed to move goods from place to place.

Using a reusable water bottle instead of a single-use bottle means less plastic used in manufacturing.

Replacing gasoline-powered cars with electric ones will reduce the use of oil.

People can also think about how much they drive. Gasoline use leads to air pollution. Driving with other people in one car instead of multiple cars reduces the amount of gasoline used. So does taking public transportation.

People can also learn about the oil and gas industry. They can find out what the industry is doing to reduce its environmental impact. Some oil and gas companies are using new technology to help the environment.

Walking or biking places can help cut down on pollution.

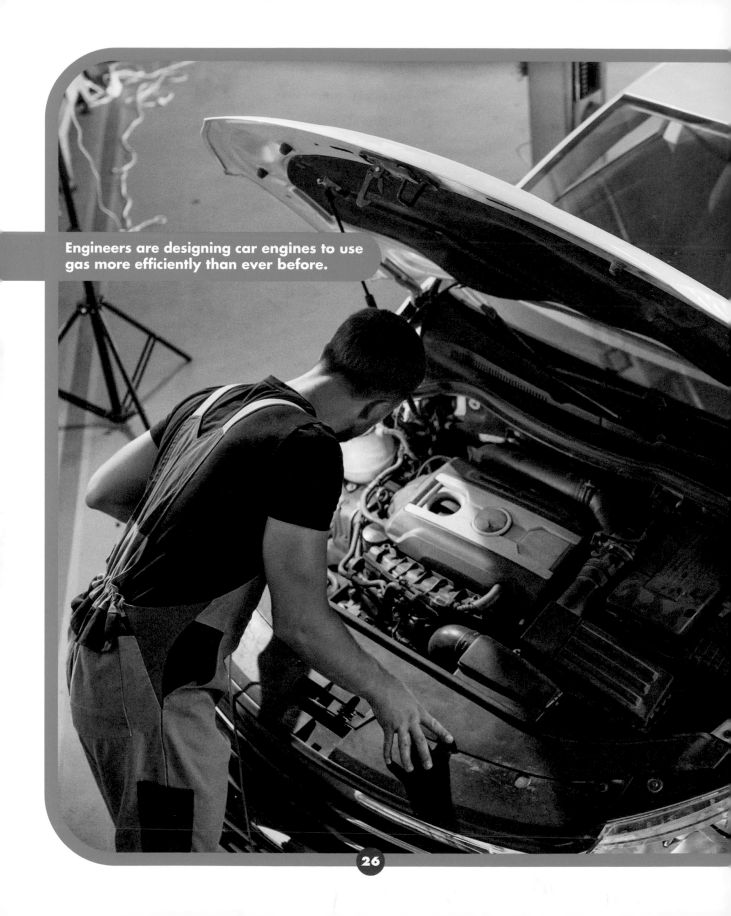

Engineers are designing car engines to use gas more efficiently than ever before.

For example, when it comes to oil **refinement**, water is a big part of the process. Some companies are working to decrease their use of fresh water and improve water recycling. Oil and gas industry leaders from around the world are also helping research renewable energy sources. Renewable energy includes wind and solar power. They hope to use current technology more efficiently while looking to the future of energy. In addition, people can write to their representatives in Congress. They can talk about any worries or ideas they have about the oil industry.

Another way oil companies and the Environmental Protection Agency are working to help the environment is through the Rigs-to-Reefs program. When old offshore oil rigs are no longer used, they can be tipped over.

ENERGY IN THE UNITED STATES
In 2020, oil made up 35 percent of the energy used in the United States. This energy was used for things such as powering vehicles, making electricity, and heating buildings. Natural gas made up 34 percent of the United States' energy. Renewable energy sources were at 12 percent, and coal was at 10 percent. Nuclear power represented 9 percent of all energy used.

Renewable energy sources, such as solar and wind power, reduce people's dependence on oil.

They settle on the sea floor. Soon, barnacles, corals, sponges, and other sea creatures attach to the rigs, creating a reef. These oil-rig reefs attract marine life. They help increase fish populations. This gives more people fishing and diving opportunities. It also helps animals find a new habitat to live in.

Understanding where oil comes from and its impacts can help everyone be more responsible when using this energy source. Supporting research on how to dig up and move oil in safer ways can benefit the environment. People can also encourage their governments to support more renewable energy options. This would reduce people's need for oil. By working together, the environment and the Earth's oil supply will be safe for generations to come.

Glossary

climate change (KLYE-mit CHAYNJ) Climate change refers to long-term changes in global temperature and weather patterns. Using oil contributes to climate change.

distilled (dih-STILLD) When oil is heated and then separated into various compounds, it has been distilled. Crude oil is distilled to get products such as gasoline.

fossil fuel (FOSS-uhl FYOO-uhl) A fossil fuel is a source of energy that comes from the remains of plants and animals that died long ago. A fossil fuel can be either coal, oil, or natural gas.

habitats (HAB-ih-tats) Habitats are places where plants and animals typically grow and live. Animal habitats can be harmed by oil spills.

pipelines (PIPE-lines) Pipelines are a series of pipes set up to move gas or oil from one place to another. Pipelines sometimes leak.

refinement (ri-FINE-ment) Refinement means to purify or take out unwanted substances from a material. Oil refinement allows people to turn oil into different products.

turbines (TUR-bines) Turbines are machines driven by water, steam, or gas passing over blades on a wheel. The turbines help create electricity.

volume (VAHL-yoom) Volume is the space an item takes up. Oil has more energy by volume than coal.

Fast Facts

- Distilling oil can make products such as gasoline and home heating oil.
- Oil is used in many products. This includes the gasoline that powers cars, planes, and trains. Oil is also used to make products such as plastic.
- Oil is a fossil fuel and a nonrenewable resource.
- Burning oil creates greenhouse gases. This warms Earth and has serious environmental impacts.
- Oil spills and leaks are dangerous to wildlife, habitats, and people.
- Many people rely on oil today.

One Stride Further

- Do you think people should continue to use oil as an energy source? Explain your answer.
- Why do you think so many people depend on oil?
- Name three ways your life would be different if you completely cut out the use of oil and products made from oil.

Find Out More

IN THE LIBRARY

Doeden, Matt. *Finding Out about Coal, Oil, and Natural Gas*. Minneapolis, MN: Lerner, 2015.

Goldish, Meish. *Oil Spill: Deepwater Horizon*. New York, NY: Bearport, 2018.

Rea, Amy C. *Natural Gas Power*. Parker, CO: The Child's World, 2023.

ON THE WEB

Visit our website for links about oil power: **childsworld.com/links**

Note to Parents, Teachers, and Librarians: We routinely verify our Web links to make sure they are safe and active sites. So encourage your readers to check them out!

Index